The Hadassahs

BLESSING EMMANUEL

THE GIRL GRACE

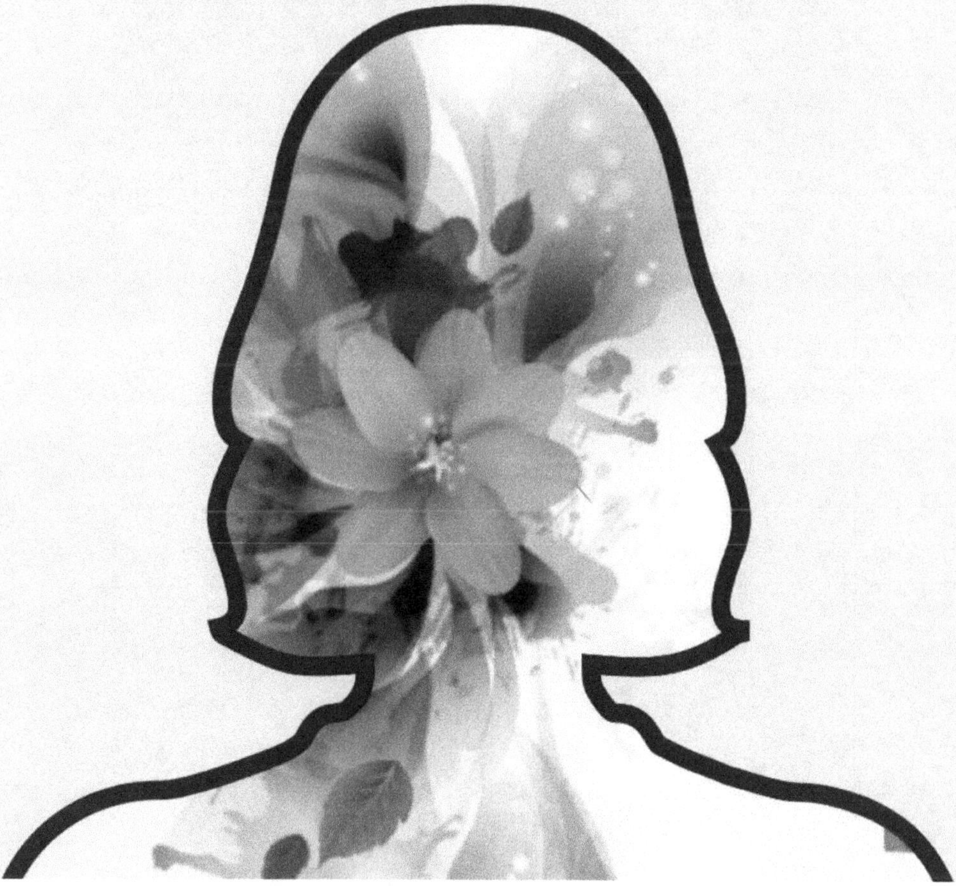

BLESSING EMMANUEL

THE GIRL GRACE

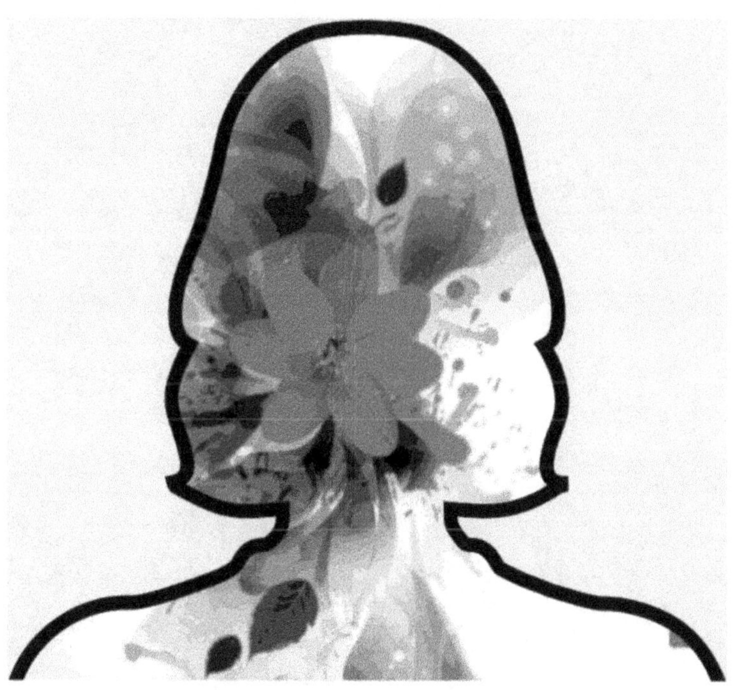

Cover Design and E-book Layout by **Andy Media** 07030827735, 08024176894

CHAPTER ONE: THE GIRL GRACE

CHAPTER ONE
THE GIRL GRACE

A girl is a special person whom God has endowed special quality abilities to do so many things.

1st Pt. 2:9 God make us to know that we are royalties, meaning we are made and created to rule in different diversification of life.

Gen. 1:28 From the beginning God has blessed us, he released his blessings declare us a born blessing therefore we should go forth and be a blessing you our generation.

GRACE

I want to establish the fact that Grace is God's undivided love towards human which will provoke immediate and divine results. An important fact to note is that Grace is not a respecter of man. Every man according to his God's giving Grace, No wonder the bible established in **"1 Corinthians 15:41"**, the different level of Grace which can also be called Glory.

Grace means – In my incapability God is not concerned but divinity will re-enforce.

Grace means not dwelling or relying on the physical but depending totally on the spiritual.

Grace means God's beautification on a man despite his short coming, forgone his past and giving meaning to his tomorrow.

Grace means upliftment without negotiation.

When grace is involve who you are or who you know is irrelevant ask **Esther**.

The Grace of God can do so many things in the life of a man
The Grace of God ca provoked open heavens
It brings favour
It put one in the track of his destiny
It makes your enemies to be at peace with you.
Grace fights the enemy without your notice.

THE GIRL GRACE

Having established who you are as a girl which include old and young, your inner capacity which can only be subdue by you alone. Let's look at Esther, who is our model in this forum.

A young girl with0ut a helper, sister, brother, mother, father working in the palace to give her a quick pass mark, first of all how did she get there? Allow me or permit me to say Grace!

Vashti grace diminishes when it was the turn of Esther grace to shine, unfortunately for queen Vashti she did not understand the prerequisite in fuelling your grace to keep burning. Nevertheless, a fresh grace has appeared and ready to blossom.

Esther came in for the contest as a normal girl not knowing what she carry inside of her, the same applies to us, everyone has been giving something special and a segment of grace has been deposited in us, we are not just ordinary we carry both the spirit, soul and body all in us and that is why we become a product of who we think we are.

Esther 2:17, what Esther came inside was waiting for the time to manifest and there the bible said ***"And she obtained grace and favour"*** what she carried made her to collect her crown, sisters we have what it takes to be great mothers, great wives, great thinkers, great in all ramification of life, therefore we need to increase our level of trust and confidence we have ourselves these lead me to.

TENDING YOUR GRACE

The devil understand that when one carry a certain level of grace, there is absolutely nothing that fellow cannot conquer and no height the fellow cannot reach therefore mocking the fulfilling of her destiny easy, therefore he plants thorns, grass around the grace to hinder it from growing, getting to that central point. And we can say that the thorns represent distractions, laziness, things that are trending, unhealthy relationships and so many others.

Esther got her crown, but she never went to sleep neither did she go to play or made numerous friends.

"Esther 4:16" she did not forget where she was coming from and what took her to the palace, she tended her grace with the water of prayer and these made her reign and talked about in whole city in Shushan in the reign of King Ahasuerus.

Therefore we tend our grace with;

1. The water of prayer, never forget as water is life so as prayer is, it gives more life to your grace helps expose the anti-grace spirit around you and puts them to shame before your face like he did to Haman.

2. The water of the word of God. The word of God is an invisible fertilizer, that gives nutrients to your grace unknowing to you, because the more you dig deep in the owner and founder of grace the more you are enlighten, strength is released, faith is poured out and then grace blossom.
   Every day you pour a cup of water of the word on your life by studying each day. It boost the grace and

make it more alive, stronger to withstand challenges, distractions, unhealthy relationships, unhealthy life it gives you the hunger to want to know more about the author of grace.

3. Doing daily checkup. Do not allow it to die, always make sure the leaves are green, never let it go day, because when it is dry it does not attract anything good, it only struggles and dies all of a sudden. You must do daily check, always say things that will boost your grace word's like – am no small, the grace of God will make me exceed limit, I must live a life of purpose the God's grace at work in my life"
   Hallelujah

CONCLUSION

The girl grace can take you the level that you did not imagine only if it is been activated by the help of the Holy Spirit.

PRAYER: Oh God I receive your grace today and I receive power to tend my grace daily. Thank you Jesus

CHAPTER TWO
THE ROYAL CROWN

For daughters of Zion royalty is not a debate because it is our birth right in Christ. God gave it to us free of change just that we get it fully through our salvation.

So for as many of you that are yet to accept him fully in your life you better act fast because the train is moving, in the kingdom there is no delay of purpose.

In our previous lesson we read a scripture in **"Gen 1:28"**, not only did God blessed us he further said we should have dominion.

For you to have dominion that means you must have a kingdom and for you to have a kingdom that means you must come from a royal family which will give you the right to reign and dominate for God to say we should have dominion that means he has placed invisible mark of royalty on our fore head, No wonder when Esther appeared before king Ahaseurus, the invisible mark of royalty on her fore head which is written boldly dominion was now made visible, and the king eyes were opened and saw the mark of royalty and said this is one of us, and these made the journey of Esther to the palace of her becoming the queen of Shushan was made easy and she received her royal crown. Every woman has a crown and a world to rule and this is the world of your purpose. You fulfilling your purpose bring out the royalty in you, your beauty unfolds and then you start reigning.

THE QUEEN'S MANDATE

As a queen you don't wear your crown and sitting idle, going to parties, lazying around, gossiping, having immoral sex, lying, and cheating. It is an abuse to the crown and shame to the kingdom and disgrace to the king, you must hold your crown in a very high esteem you must value it, therefore you must seek to know what the king like, remember vashti she had her crown, but she lost it eventually, pride and disobedience collected her crown in just a day, she never believed her crown would be taken, she forgot that in the kingdom there is principles and law guiding the kingdom when is violated sometimes it can be dangerous and cost you more than you can imagine.

Vashti failed to understand what the king like, she has with the king, eat with the king but still fail to understand the king, what makes him happy and other likes, she was too familiar with the king, she felt she has known him all, she thought beauty is enough to keep the kingdom and please the king.

Now to us, sometimes we also feel we have known God a lot because we go to church every day, help the poor, give our offerings and such like, but it is never enough. When the time for vashti understanding of the king was to be tested she failed in just one sitting.

Sadly enough she was not given a second chance and her crown was retrieved, she could not fulfill her mandate, she failed in the kingdom and was driven like an ordinary person.

NOW THE MANDATE

- As a queen that you are, everyday you must seek to please your king (God) like what he likes and hate what he hates.

Until you are ready and able to please your king fulfilling mandate will be difficult, it should be you first mandate and priority to please your king, don't get too familiar with him, remember what it cost vashti,, her's was disobedience, what is your own, is it fornication, adultery, love of money, love of material things, backbiting, jealousy and others.

Please him not looking at your neighbor, what you will get in return, your status, your beauty but because of the crown on you which you will not want to lose for anything and for the king sake.

- As a queen that is Royalty you must be

different, dare to be different. The kingdom is only for a selected few, and these few looked out for because of what they carry inside the mark of Royalty on their fore-head they are known because they are always different from, in the crowd, you must not join them, you must not behave like them even when you want to do things it must be done moderately. Always remind yourself of who you are, never forget that you have a kingdom and a king to please.

- You must be an Ambassador

A queen always represents her kingdom so as not to put the king to shame. A queen must be a role model therefore all things must be done moderately, eating, dressing, talking e.t.c.

As an ambassador and a queen with the crown never forget to always look good never forget that you are coming from the royal family, the king should always be pleased with your outwork, and the glory of your inside will be reflected in your outside.

- The mandate of increase, the kingdom must not be small, people must hear about the kingdom, they must not be small, people must hear about the kingdom, they must want to join the kingdom, it has to be established in different areas "Esther4:16b" she brought in her maidens, think of ways to increase the kingdom.

CONCLUSION

God has given each and everyone an assignment; you must go and ask God your assignment on this earth, make sure you do it so you will not lose your crown at the end.

PRAYERS

Father, open my eyes to know what to do at every given time of my life. **So** help me God Amen.

CHAPTER THREE

THE PRCE

Once upon a time in the life of a young girl, she decided to save little money, little money so at the end of the day she will have a reasonable cash to pay for her jamb fees, after saving for close to a year when the money was up to the figure she was expecting she called the person she will be giving the money to and the person told her to go and pay the money in his account the following day because is almost late, okay sir she said.

The next day, she woke up so early so she can go to the bank before attending to other things. So she quickly dress up and off she go, on arriving at the bank, grin grin her phone rang, she picked up the phone and lo her sister, so she quickly answer pondering why she called so early, on answering the call, the sister started crying, what happened she asked, Big sis. Mum is critically ill and she has been rushed to the hospital and the doctor said money has to be deposited for treatment to begin. Sis please do something before we lost mum. She hanged up the call. Oh no she look at herself, the money and looked at where she was standing at the front of the bank to deposit the cash for her jamb exam, she paused a bit and asked herself life and jamb which is better and she made a big decision, she left the bank threw away the receipt and went home to see the mum at the hospital, she paid the doctor and treatment started the mum life was saved but she lost her jamb.

The price is a painful word that most person don't want to hear, how can I forget this, how can I forget that, it is very costly and that is why it is called a price. And I boldly say in this present generation if you must fulfill mandate you must pay the price, if you must like a life of purpose, you must be ready to pay a price.

- **WHAT IS PRICE?**
  Something you give in exchange to get what you want. Every level of greatness in life comes with different price tags. The higher the purpose, the higher the price to pay, every price you pay leads you to the next price to pay until you get to your finish line and of course you know your finish line is

death. Joseph paid different price before he was qualified to be in the palace to get to where he got in his time. Our model queen Esther she paid a big price. In Esther chapter “4” when the task was given to her, it was too big because she knows the consequence which is death she declined, but when she realized another side of the consequence on her people, then a price must be paid. Remember the kingdom will not always be rosy, the given must be prepared at all times so as not to be caught unaware.

Also if you pay the price you receive your reward, if you don’t pay the price you will also receive your reward.

Now you must pay the price of -

- **THE PRICE OF SALVATION**

  You must be fully pant of the kingdom not only with your words but with your heart, the price to receive genuine salvation, you must build true relationship with your king, know him, not the knowing your pastor told you, but your personal knowing let it be intimate, now ask yourself do I have an intimate relationship with my king? When a man and woman wants to have and intimate relationship you know how it feels, feel so good, lovely sweet, heaven on earth, this should be same as your king (God) a moment when you just want to be alone with him, this lead me to the next price.

- **THE PRICE OF TIME**

  You cannot build relationship if you can't create time, they say time and communication is one of the bedrock for the growth of any relationship, God our king has given us 24 hours in a day, you must remove some minutes or hour to be intimate with him. If you don't have time for your king (God) something else will fill up that time and you gradually forget your root and become a mere talker without a solid backup.

  The price of time will make you to study his word because you want to know your king more personally. The price of time will make you want to pray more because you want to hear the voice of your king and he should listen to yours too, make him your final and the relationship will be sweet and rewarding.

- **THE PRICE OF DETERMINATION**

  Determination, to serve to stand for the truth, to have faith, to trust totally. You have first decide in your heart if you are ready to pay the price because some things you must let go, some attitudes, life style, friends – your circle of friends and others. You must come to a conclusion in your heart that you must live your life each day as if this is your last day on earth, meaning you must have the consciousness of Hell and Heaven reality in you.

You must tell yourself if I don't go to hell then I must go heaven and if I must go to heaven I must live according heaven standard and not the world standard, you must not be moved by what people say but by what God have said over you, so therefore your intimacy with him must not be broken or disrupted by friends, sex, lies, jealousy, malice, parties, fashions, immoral behaviors lots more.

You must make a decision. Esther said "if I perish I perish" Joseph said "How can I do this great wickedness and sin against God and my master".

Queens that rule, Queens that are purposeful always make the decisions that will please the King (God).

CONCLUSION

The price is very costly and demanding, you need

more of God's daily grace to pay the price daily because it is continuous until we reach the finish line (death).

PRAYER

Please Lord I want to pay the price, but I can't do it on my own, therefore I need your Grace in my life in Jesus name Amen.

So much power lies in the words of the king so as to the queen, the kingdom is filled with power. **Luke 10:19** "behold I give unto you power to thread upon serpents and scorpions and over all the powers of the enemy, and nothing shall by means hurt you".

From the beginning, the devil has been fighting tirelessly over the authority given, he won at the beginning through woman, and the authority was taken and we were driven from the kingdom. The devil understood the authenticity of this power that's why she started fighting for man not to fully get access to it right from inception. The kingdom is never a place to play around; those in the kingdom are serious minded people. God has gone us that authority we lost through his son Jesus by grace in **Psalms 24:1-9** he demanded for the keys of the kingdom that was taken.

The royal authority gives you an edge over the kingdom of darkness that is why you must exercise this authority on a daily basis. Authority is not only claimed it is activated by declaration.

HOW CAN YOU EXERCISE THIS AUTHORITY

1. **BEEN A MEMBER OF THE KINGDOM**
   An outsider cannot dictate what happens in the inside, the president of America cannot give the final

decision on the matter that concerns Nigeria because someone is also and has been placed to oversee the affairs of Nigeria. So as to the kingdom, for you to exercise authority you must be recognized. Your actions must speak more volume, the queen in her kingdom have the power to make decision that will stand. You must make a solid and concrete decision this year if you really want to be a full part of the kingdom what you just need is a gate fee of you salvation and you will be allowed in. and you cannot be mesmerized in your kingdom because you are backed up by a greater force.

2. **ON YOUR KNEES**

As a queen your beauty is not only needed, neither your skills your powerful tool or weapon is your knees; you must know how to bow your knees. Battles are won on your knees; you take authority on your knees. You must be that praying woman, you make up is not enough your royal apparels are not enough, because you are on a battle ground and you cannot afford to be caught unarmed.

Intercede for the kingdom, you must always stand in between, be a watchman of your home, too much sleep destroys the power. Always be alert "**John 10:10**". Prayers are stored for the stormy days. Our model even Esther, in **Esther 4:16**. Even in the palace she didn't forgot where she was coming from, she remembered that the knee is very powerful as to maintain authority and be in change; she used the power of the knees to conquer Haman and restored the joy of her people and their freedom. Don't be too relax, when you sense victory is around then you pray harder. You don't take charge by gossiping, murmuring, complaining you settle the matter silently in your closet on your knees. You must be that praying woman.

3. **YOUR TONGUE (Proverbs 31:26)**

The tongue is one powerful tool to exercise authority, life and death lies in the tongue. Where the word of the king is, there's power **Eccl. 8:4**. Store words in the spirit, which will produce for you the right harvest at the appointed time. When you make use of your tongue talking you are addressing circumstances, and situations effecting positive changes in your life and future. When you talk you release energy in the realm of spirit.

Don't use your tongue wrongly declare the word, decree things to be using authority and boldness, don't forget you are royalty and there is power in your words. So do not speak negative words, don't let the enemy of the kingdom hear you speak wrongly, instead use your tongue to shape your world positively, keep saying the right words don't stop until you see it manifest physically.

CONCLUSION

The royal authority is not for fun nor for jamboree but to be used to settle stubborn matters affecting the kingdom, therefore you must not allow anyone or anything to take away your authority from you because it gives you an edge over the enemies.

PRAYERS

Father I take change, I take authority through the name of Jesus am above only my right cannot be taken from me in Jesus name Amen.

Illllllllllllllllllllllllllllllllllllllllllllllllllllllllllllllllllllllll
lllll

CHAPTER FIVE THE HONtE BUILDER

Illllllllllllllllllllllllllllllllllllllllllllllllllllllllllllllllllllllll
lllll

The woman has the power to build her home and also has the power to scatter her home, I believe God gave the woman the sixth sense, which God did not give to man, this often called the women intuition, God has given you the wisdom to be the builders, not the head of the home. But the builders, the organizers, the goal-getters, there are some great qualities instill in us as royalties, which differentiate our home from the "outsiders home" this make us to be an example to follow.

A builder, he gets the chance of the type and design of house he would need through the architecture, he draws the plan of the house, giving the different demarcations on the different rooms, and therefore he has a direction through the drawing. So as to the Royalties, you need to have a picture of the kind of home you want to live in and you will be the one to create it; do you want it to be a Christ-like home or a just ordinary home you will make the decision.

After the written down drawing of the building, then the builders go to work, you need and must work it out, you must go to work by been the ideal woman first that will fit in the home you envisage.

BEEN SPIRITUALLY ALERT

Don't only be a fashionister be a far-spiritual, the battle is never ending therefore you must not be tired or be caught unaware. Don't feed your flesh alone, don't dress your body alone, don't wear the makeover alone, and don't look good alone. Always remember to first feed, dress and take care of your spiritual life first because the spiritual controls the physical.

Do not be carried away by the trends and pleasures of this world, focus on retaining the standard of building a Christian home, don't be too busy to pray, study God's word, give to the needy, evangelize, do not fall out from the presence of the God because you will only live but, what will you live belief "always store prayers in your bank. It should not be empty they speak for you even when you are tired to pray or study.

THEY TAKE AND SEEK DIRECTION FROM GOD (KING)

Right direction leads you to your destination in life, you ask direction, what neat they to do, what actions to take what steps to take. The builder will not just go and be building he gets direction from his master the owner of the building, the same applies to us, how you can build what you don't know. Leaving beside the owner and the founder of the home that's why you must work in hand with the owner of the building. As the king wants the queen to be close to him, so as God wants us to be close to him, the more you get close to him, the more of him you know and the direction is given to you.

WISDOM IS THE PRINCIPAL THING:

A Queen that operates with God's wisdom cannot be thrown here or there, inside gives you an edge over your enemy wisdom which is the night application of knowledge, wisdom helps you towards your reactions to tings the **Proverb 31** woman adorned herself, with God's wisdom.

NEVER FORGET TO ALWAYS ASK FOR DIVINE WISDOM

- Let your mouth be filled with wisdom through the word of God, do not fill your mouth with curse, lying and all manner of things rather fill yourself with more of God's word
- The fear of the Lord: **Prov. 30:31**. A woman that fears the Lord shall be praised; you can't rule a kingdom without the fear for the owner of the kingdom. The fear of the Lord must be your first priority, by the fear you have for him, you will carry

out his instructions dutifully, this fear will make you not only be as church goer but to be his secret lover, there must be a scheduled time with him. Queens build they don't scatter, no wonder when the family of Esther wanted to scatter (the Jews) Esther had to stand in the gap. **Eccl 12:13** the whole conclusion of our existence as human's and most of all as Royalties is to fear God and keep his commandments.

CONCLUSION

The fear of God is the beginning of great wisdom that will lead you in becoming a great home builder and not a scatterer. Depend on God for grace.

PRAYER

Father releases upon me the special grace to be a heaven home builder on earth. Amen.

CHAPTER SIX
A PURPOSE LIFE

The whole existence of man is to live a purposeful life, how can you live without being felt even in you Jerusalem, no human is empty, we are on our different race with different specific assignment through which the kingdom of darkness will be depopulated and gives more population in the kingdom of heaven. Then the word of the Lord came to Jeremiah in **Jer. 1:5,** and God told him his purpose to be a prophet to his generations you can't expect Jeremiah to go and become a singer, or a drummer his assignment is specific you are called to be a prophet in your generation.

As a given you must know why you are in the kingdom, not only to wear new clothes, to brace ourselves with jewelries, good hair and the rests, they are all good but they are not your primary assignment on earth. Esther was in the kingdom for a valid reason which she fulfilled, she was meant to deliver her people from the hands of Haman, thou is was not an easy task, but that was the assignment, every task and challenges that we encounter in the journey, God has given us the capability to bear and overcome those challenges. The task he gives you, he also gives you the grace to carry it out and do it accurately only if the person I willing and ready, every test you encounter in the journey of life leads you to the next test. These build you and make your faith stronger.

Every mathematical problem has an equation that will help in solving such problem, each mathematical problem with its own equation, for every task we go through there is always a means of escape and is has its own solution. Therefore inside the problem there is the solution.

THE PURPOSEFUL WOMAN

A woman of courage and determination who takes deliberate action to empower herself to achieve her goals. A woman who knows what she wants, she is clear on what is important and where she wants to go. "There no greater gift than to honor your life's calling. It's why you were born. And how you become must truly alive"– "OPRAH WINFREY".

We can say that a man without purpose is like a car driving without destination. Purpose makes one focus. Purpose can be seen as your timc originality. We can also say purpose is our God given assignment on earth. God brought Esther to the palace because there was a purpose she must fulfill. What if Esther was not the queen of Shushan, what would have happened to the Jews that was in that land. God did not only brought someone that is a Jew to be the queen, but someone that is ready to pay the price so that purpose can be fulfilled.

There are thousands girls that are beautiful, yes they have the body, the shape and whatever you can think of. But God was looking for someone that can stand in the gap that has the heart to do whatever it takes just to fulfill heaven purpose for their lives. When purpose is identified beauty will find more expression. What can be found in God, with God and through God "Purpose"

CONCLUSION

To live a purposeful life means you have a clear goal, a clear vision and you don't get distracted by other minor things that less matter.

PRAYER

Father, open my eyes to see more of your purpose for me. Help me to fulfill purpose.

ABOUT THE BOOK

In the GIRL GRACE, a practical essence of woman is discussed. This book explains that the girl is more than what she thinks and can achieve Greater not minding the present circumstances and distractions. God has endowed us with lots of potentials which when use positively produce a life results impacting and been a model to others.

This Book Reminds us that women are a precious gift from God to the world.

Also, in this book we will discover that we are queens and we have a Kingdom to protect. We are also reminded that we have a purpose to fulfill in the kingdom, we are not there for formality but to make positive impact because the king's business requires haste. Just like Esther our Model who stood in the gap for her people.

ABOUT THE AUTHOR

BLESSING EMMANUEL is a teacher of God's word, a writer, a singer, a speaker, the founder of THE HADASSAHS a group specifically for sisters, where we discussed God's word, pray and address life issues, She is devoted in impacting in the lives of sisters reminding them of who they truly are through God's word and the help of the Holy Spirit. Let's enjoy this ride of Grace as we sail..